W9-AZC-290

921
ROD

Rappoport, Ken.

Super sports star
Alex Rodriguez.

$23.93   35360030013145

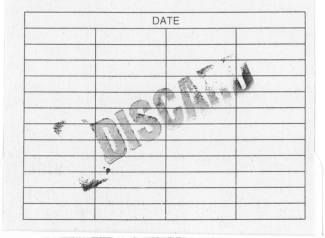

DATE			

0.5

BAKER & TAYLOR

SUPER SPORTS ★ STAR
ALEX RODRIGUEZ

Ken Rappoport

Enslow Publishers, Inc.

40 Industrial Road	PO Box 38
Box 398	Aldershot
Berkeley Heights, NJ 07922	Hants GU12 6BP
USA	UK

http://www.enslow.com

Library of Congress Cataloging-in-Publication Data

Rappoport, Ken.
    Super sports star Alex Rodriguez / Ken Rappoport.
        p. cm. — (Super sports star)
    Summary: Surveys the life and career of Texas Rangers shortstop Alex Rodriguez, a natural athlete who, in 2001, became the highest paid player in baseball.
    Includes bibliographical references and index.
    ISBN 0-7660-2138-6
    1. Rodriguez, Alex, 1975– Juvenile literature. 2. Baseball players—United States—Biography—Juvenile literature. [1. Rodriguez, Alex, 1975– 2. Baseball players. 3. Dominican Americans—Biography.] I. Title. II. Series.
    GV865.R62R36 2004
    796.357'092—dc21   2003011124

Printed in the United States of America

10 9 8 7 6 5 4 3 2 1

To Our Readers:
We have done our best to make sure all Internet Addresses in this book were active and appropriate when we went to press. However, the author and the publisher have no control over and assume no liability for the material available on those Internet sites or on other Web sites they may link to. Any comments or suggestions can be sent by e-mail to comments@enslow.com or to the address on the back cover.

Photo Credits: © 2002 David Durochik/MLB Photos, pp. 6, 11; © 1999 Allen Kee/MLB Photos, p. 19; © Brad Mangin/MLB Photos, p. 25; © 2000 Brad Mangin/MLB Photos, p. 32; © 2001 Brad Mangin/MLB Photos, p. 14; © 2001 Rich Pilling/MLB Photos, p. 34; © 2002 Rich Pilling/MLB Photos, pp. 9, 39; © 1996 John Reid III/MLB Photos, p. 17; © 2000 John H. Reid III/MLB Photos, p. 27; © 1999 Ben Van Houten/MLB Photos, p. 30; © Williamson/MLB Photos, p. 44; © 2002 Williamson/MLB Photos, p. 37; © 2001 John Williamson/MLB Photos, p. 1; © 2002 John Williamson/MLB Photos, p. 4; © Michael Zagaris/MLB Photos, p. 22.

Cover Photo: © 2001 John Williamson/MLB Photos.

CONTENTS

Introduction

Alex Rodriguez is baseball's "252 Million Dollar Man." He is the highest paid player in the game. The Texas Rangers signed Rodriguez to a $252 million deal for ten years. He is a shortstop for the Texas Rangers.

Alex Rodriguez is big and strong. He covers a lot of ground with his long legs and he has a powerful arm. He hits for a high average. He hits for power and already holds many batting records for shortstops.

He is one of baseball's nicest stars. He finds time to sign autographs. He likes to talk to fans. Rodriguez is thankful he can be paid to play the game he has loved since he was a kid.

He worked very hard to become a star, reaching the top as fast as he could run around the bases.

CHAPTER 1

The $252 Million Man

All eyes were on Alex Rodriguez as he stepped to the plate. It was the 2001 season. Rodriguez was the talk of baseball. He had signed a big contract with the Texas Rangers.

Now he was batting against the Minnesota Twins. The Twins' fans were booing him. It was nothing new. "The volume has gone up a little bit on the Boo-O-Meter," Rodriguez said.

Why were the fans booing? They thought Rodriguez made too much money. That meant higher ticket prices. The fans had to pay more money to see baseball games.

Fans made fun of his nickname, "A-Rod." In Seattle they held up signs. They said "A-WAD" and "PAY-ROD." They threw fake money on the field.

It was hard to argue against Rodriguez as a ballplayer. In 2001 many thought he was the best in the game. He was a shortstop with awesome power. But was one baseball player worth so much money? That was the hot topic on every sports talk show across America.

The only way Rodriguez could stop the fans from booing was with his bat. And he had done that often enough. When he visited Minnesota in late August, Rodriguez had already hit 39 home runs.

Rodriguez stepped into the batter's box in the first inning. A runner led off base. The boos were still ringing in his ears. He swung hard at a belt-high fastball. The ball came off his bat like a shot. It soared toward left-center field. Going . . . going . . . gone. Home run! The blast had cleared the wall more than 400 feet away.

Earlier that month Rodriguez had stopped the booing at Yankee Stadium with a home run. Now he had done it again. The Rangers beat the Twins, 10–1. His home run moved Rodriguez into a special class. He became only the ninth player to reach the 40-homer level in four straight seasons.

Alex Rodriguez shows the fans he can hit home runs.

Alex Rodriguez was now playing under a bigger spotlight because of his contract. But nothing had changed. He was still hitting the ball out of the park just as he had for many years.

The Next Cal Ripken

Alexander Emmanuel Rodriguez had come a long way. He was born in New York City on July 27, 1975. He grew up around baseball in the Dominica Republic and Miami, Florida. Alex's father, Victor, had played pro baseball, and he taught Alex to love the game. Alex's brother, Joe, taught him something just as important. "He pitched to me in our games and he'd always let me win—until the end of the game," Rodriguez said. "Then he'd go on and beat me. It made me want to get better."

Alex also has a sister, Susy. She helped him with his schoolwork. Their father left the family when Alex was ten. His mother, Lourdes, worked hard to support the family. "It was hard," Rodriguez said. "I did my best to help out around the house and bring home good grades to make my mom proud."

Sports came naturally. He played baseball, football, and basketball. But Alex was not always a star. In his first year on the high school baseball team, Alex had a tough time. His coach told Alex he needed to get stronger. He lifted weights. Every day he did 100 push-ups and 100 sit-ups. Soon he was one of the best high school players in America. Major-league teams suddenly showed interest.

Every year, major-league teams pick players from high school and college. Many thought Rodriguez would be the first pick. He played for Miami Westminster Christian High School. He was the national high school Player of the Year. Alex had led his team to the national championship.

★ ★ ★ UP CLOSE

Along with baseball, Alex Rodriguez also starred as a football player in high school. As quarterback for the Miami Westminster Christian High School team, he helped to set a school record for touchdowns.

Rodriguez
was not
always a star
at baseball.
He had to
work very
hard to get
to where he
is today.

He was called another Cal Ripken, Jr. That was just fine with Rodriguez. The great Baltimore Orioles' shortstop was his hero. Like Ripken, Rodriguez was tall, quick, and graceful. He covered a lot of ground at shortstop. He had a good glove, a strong arm, and he could hit with power.

Ever since Little League, Alex tried to play just like Ripken. He copied the way Ripken played shortstop and he copied the way Ripken hit. He kept the player's poster over his bed. One day Alex actually met his hero. They were introduced during spring training. Alex was already a high school star. Ripken was impressed. "My first impression was that he was physically mature," Ripken said. "I assumed he'd be a little meek and underdeveloped."

After Alex completed his senior season there was more excitement to come. On June 3, 1993, he waited for a phone call. Alex was not alone. A group of friends, family, and reporters was at his home in Miami, Florida. They were all waiting. Which team would select Rodriguez in the 1993 baseball draft?

Finally the phone rang. It was the Seattle Mariners. They had made Alex the top pick! At the age of seventeen Alex Rodriguez was on his way to the pros.

Money Player

Everyone was watching Alex Rodriguez. He had received a $1.36 million signing bonus from the Mariners. It was more money than teams usually give players just out of high school. Could he handle the pressure?

"The main thing they are looking at is how I play," Rodriguez said. "Do I play hard? Do I play like I have money? I don't care how much money I have. I'm working hard. I'm not saving myself for tomorrow, that's for sure."

Rodriguez started his pro career with a bang. In his very first week he slammed a 440-foot home run. He was playing for the Appleton Foxes of the Class A Midwest League in the minor leagues. Rodriguez quickly became one of the league's top players.

Everywhere Rodriguez went, people wanted to talk to him and take his picture. Reporters wanted to talk to baseball's new

Rodriguez started his major-league career with the Seattle Mariners. But first it was off to the minor leagues.

wonder boy. Photographers wanted to snap his picture. Rodriguez was on the fast track to the major leagues.

Rodriguez moved up to Jacksonville (Florida) in a Class AA league. In his very first at bat there, he hit a home run.

Then he went to Calgary (Canada). Rodriguez was playing in Triple-A. It was the highest level of minor-league ball. There, Rodriguez ran into problems. He called home. "I was hitting about .200 and I said, 'Mom, I'm tired. I want to come home.' She said, 'I don't want you home with that attitude. Whether you have a month left or three months, you go out and play hard.'"

In the final week of the season, Calgary was tied 3–3 with Tacoma in the 10th inning. Rodriguez stepped to the plate with a man on base. He took a cut and connected. The ball rose higher and higher. Home run! Calgary won, 5–3. Rodriguez had found his stroke again.

By the time his first pro season was over,

he had played in all three levels of minor-league ball. The Mariners brought him up in 1994 to get a taste of the big leagues. He was only eighteen years old. In all, he played 125 games for four teams over five months. He had visited sixteen states and Canada. Not even a broken nose could keep him out of action. "That's a tough road," he said. "I've learned a lot about professional baseball along the way."

Rodriguez was tired. He could have used a vacation. Instead he headed south to play winter ball. There he would get more practice. He would also learn more about himself.

A Career Year

Alex Rodriguez was excited. He tightened his seat belt as the plane dipped its wings. The airfield was straight ahead. Out of the window he could see the island glistening in the sun. He felt he was going home.

The Dominican Republic is a small island nation in the Caribbean Sea. It is a few hundred miles off the United States coast. Its hot weather makes it excellent for playing baseball all year.

Rodriguez had two reasons for going there. He would be playing in one of the top winter leagues. He also would be going back to his family roots. His parents were born in the Dominican Republic and he had lived there as a young boy.

"Coming here meant more than working on hitting a curve or the backhand play in the hole," Rodriguez said. "I came to find out where I'm from."

Rodriguez played for a team called Escogido Leones. It was a real test. He faced top pro pitchers. He had a hard time hitting. Alex's batting average was low. He only hit about .200, but he impressed everyone with his great fielding at shortstop and his great attitude. Rodriguez's manager and coaches liked how hard he worked. So did the fans. He became one of the most popular players in the league. "All I wanted here was not to embarrass myself," Rodriguez said.

★★★ UP CLOSE

Alex Rodriguez speaks two languages, English and Spanish. He was born in New York City and grew up in Miami, Florida, after a short time in the Dominican Republic.

In 1995 he played in 48 games for the Mariners. He also played in the minors. In 1996 Rodriguez was in spring training. He walked up to Mariners manager Lou Piniella. "I'm ready," Rodriguez said.

"I know you are, son," the Mariners manager answered.

By the 1996 season, Alex Rodriguez was ready to play major-league ball full-time.

He named Rodriguez as his starting shortstop. Alex Rodriguez was only twenty years old. He had played in only 65 major-league games. He was one of the youngest ever to start at short in the majors. And by midseason he was among the AL batting leaders. He was also on the All-Star team. And he was on the cover of *Sports Illustrated*. He was called "The Game's Next Superstar."

Rodriguez finished with a .358 batting average. It was the highest average in the majors. It was also the highest for a right-handed batter since Joe DiMaggio in 1939. Rodriguez's power numbers were amazing for a shortstop. He hit 36 home runs. He set five hitting records for shortstops. He knocked in 123 runs and scored 141. He only made 15 errors. He was named the Sporting News Player of the Year. He finished second in the Most Valuable Player voting. All this, in just his first full season in the majors.

What was next?

Making More History

Look out, Rico Petrocelli! It would only be a matter of time before Alex Rodriguez broke Petrocelli's season home run record for American League shortstops. That is what everyone said. Petrocelli hit 40 home runs for Boston in 1969. That was six years before Rodriguez was born.

At the age of twenty-one, Rodriguez was already one of the top hitters in the game. Once at Yankee Stadium the pitcher tried to blow a fastball past Rodriguez. He hit the pitch into the center field bleachers. Only nine other players had done so. Another time Rodriguez hit a huge home run at Toronto's SkyDome. That one went 450 feet.

Then Rodriguez ran into trouble. Suddenly, he was out of the lineup with injuries. He missed 21 games in the 1997 season. He was unable to keep up his home run pace. His batting average slipped.

The Mariners were still fighting for a playoff berth. Late in the season they faced Anaheim. Rodriguez turned his ankle. He refused to leave the game and kept playing. His team won. The Mariners were division champions!

The 1997 season ended in a playoff loss. It was an up and down season for Rodriguez.

★ UP CLOSE

Alex Rodriguez loves computer games. When he played for the Seattle Mariners he enjoyed challenging Ken Griffey Jr. When he has spare time, Rodriguez also likes to read, play golf, and go fishing.

In 1998 Rodriguez was back to full health. So was his home run swing. He was named to the All-Star team. He hit a home run to help the AL win.

Rodriguez's home run total climbed. It was the last month of the season. He was just one home run away from Rico Petrocelli's record.

Rodriguez was one home run away from breaking a record. Could he do it?

But Rodriguez's bat went cold. Game after game went by with no home runs.

When Rodriguez stepped in against Anaheim he had not hit a home run in twelve days. He worked the count to three balls and one strike. Rodriguez swung on the next pitch. He sent it over the right field fence. He had tied the record! Alex Rodriguez joined a special group. He became only the third player with 40 home runs and 40 steals in the same season.

Three days later Rodriguez hit another home run to break the record. Later in the season he hit one more for a total of 42. What a power show!

In 1999 he hit 42 again. He did it even though he missed 33 games. It made him the first shortstop in AL history to hit as many as 40 homers in a season twice.

There were other great hitting shortstops in the big leagues. But none had matched Rodriguez's home run totals.

Awesome Alex

Rodriguez was struggling. It was late in the 2000 season. He was in the worst slump of his career. "He's been chasing bad pitches," Seattle manager Lou Piniella said. "Maybe he's been trying to do too much."

Rodriguez was on his way to a third straight season of 40 home runs. In September his bat went cold again. It was a bad time for him to go into a slump. It was the final weekend of the season. The Mariners were in a fight for a playoff berth. "We need Alex to get hot," the manager said.

On Friday night his team lost. When Rodriguez stepped to the plate the next night he was still stuck on 38 home runs. He had not hit one into the seats in 42 at bats.

Rodriguez dug into the batter's box. He waited for the pitch. He swung and the ball sailed over the wall for a home run. It was

Alex
Rodriguez
plays
great
baseball.

number 39. Later in the game he hit another—number 40. Rodriguez smashed four hits in all. He knocked in seven runs. His team beat Anaheim, 21–9. It was big. As Rodriguez ran around the bases after his second home run he held up his arms. He balled his fists. It was a rare show of emotion for the usually quiet shortstop. "It was my 40th and it kind of broke the game open," he said. "So it was very good timing."

Now it was Sunday. The Mariners had to win to make the playoffs. But they were in trouble. They fell behind 2–0 in the first inning. Rodriguez hit a homer. His team rallied to beat Anaheim. The Mariners were in the playoffs! "We showed guts, knowing we had to win two games on the road after that ugly game Friday night," Rodriguez said. "It was like Games 6 and 7 of a World Series. That's why you see everyone like this."

In the first round of the playoffs, the Mariners beat Chicago. They advanced to the AL Championship series against New York. Rodriguez was a hitting hero for Seattle. Even so, the Mariners lost the playoff series to the Yankees.

Was that Rodriguez's last time in a Mariners uniform? That was the big question in Seattle. Rodriguez would be a free agent after the season. He had completed the final year of his contract. He could now sign with any team in baseball.

One thing was certain. Wherever Rodriguez played he would be paid a lot of money. It was the biggest story in sports. Which team would sign him?

Striking it Rich

Alex Rodriguez had to pinch himself. Was it real? "I never dreamed in my wildest dreams I would be making this type of money," he said.

Rodriguez had just signed an amazing $252 million contract with the Texas Rangers for ten years. He used some of the money to help others. Rodriguez gave about $4 million to the University of Miami. He started the Alex Rodriguez Foundation to help raise money for the Boys and Girls Clubs. He works with them in Miami, Florida, and the Dallas-Fort Worth area in Texas. He is the group's national spokesman. The clubs help to make children's lives better.

Alex Rodriguez loves to work with children. When he has spare time, he also likes to go boating and play golf and basketball. In November 2002, he married his longtime girlfriend, Cynthia Scurtis.

After the 2000 season, Alex Rodriguez became a free agent. He signed with the Texas Rangers.

The $252 million contract was the talk of the sports world. Now all Rodriguez had to do was live up to it. "This is going to be a very challenging year," he said.

On Opening Day Rodriguez was far from perfect. He made a throwing error. He slipped and fell while trying to complete a double play. And he did not hit the ball very far.

His slump continued. It brought back an awful memory from high school. He made an error in his senior year that cost his team the state title. He cried after the game. "It's always in my mind," he said. "That's why I don't take anything for granted."

After his first 10 games of the 2001 season he was still looking for his first home run. He had only knocked in two runs.

Finally, Rodriguez came to life in a three-game series against Oakland. He blasted four home runs and knocked in 11 runs. The Rangers swept the series. Alex Rodriguez was named the AL's Player of the Week.

Rodriguez had again found his home run swing. In the final weeks of the season an important record was within his reach. In 1958 Ernie Banks had hit 47 home runs. It was the major-league record for shortstops.

The Rangers were already out of the pennant race. All eyes were now on Rodriguez's race for the home run record. His team led Anaheim 5–2 when he stepped to the plate in the fifth inning. The pitcher fired and Rodriguez swung. The crowd started to roar as the ball sailed toward the right field seats. Home run! Rodriguez had tied the record with number 47. Two days later he hit number 48 to break the record. Rodriguez finished the season with 52 homers.

That would be hard to top. But leave it to Rodriguez to top himself.

★★★ UP CLOSE

When Alex Rodriguez hit 57 home runs in 2002 he joined Ernie Banks as the only shortstops in major-league history with four straight seasons of 40 or more homers. Banks set the standard from 1957–60 with the Chicago Cubs.

In 2002 he hit 57 home runs. He knocked in 142 runs. Both were career highs. He was selected the American League's Player of the Year. That was important to Rodriguez. He had been picked by his fellow players.

In 2003, Rodriguez was again among the top home-run hitters in baseball. One team general manager called him "the best shortstop ever."

Rodriguez's contract had put him in a special class. He was under great pressure to live up to it. And he did! Playing for a new team, a new manager, and with new teammates, Alex Rodriguez started his time in Texas with two of the greatest seasons in baseball history.

No wonder he is called the greatest player in the game.

CAREER STATISTICS

				🏏 MLB								
Year	Team	G	AB	R	H	2B	3B	HR	RBI	BB	SB	Avg.
1994	Seattle	17	54	4	11	0	0	0	2	3	3	.204
1995	Seattle	48	142	15	33	6	2	5	19	6	4	.232
1996	Seattle	146	601	141	215	54	1	36	123	59	15	.358
1997	Seattle	141	587	100	176	40	3	23	84	41	29	.300
1998	Seattle	161	686	123	213	35	5	42	124	45	46	.310
1999	Seattle	129	502	110	143	25	0	42	111	56	21	.285
2000	Seattle	148	554	134	175	34	2	41	132	100	15	.316
2001	Texas	162	632	133	201	34	1	52	135	75	18	.318
2002	Texas	162	624	125	187	27	2	57	142	87	9	.300
Total		1,114	4,382	885	1,354	255	16	298	872	472	160	.309

G—Games
AB—At Bats
R—Runs
H—Hits
2B—Doubles
3B—Triples

HR—Home Runs
RBI—Runs Batted In
BB—Bases on Balls (Walks)
SB—Stolen Bases
Avg.—Batting Average

Where to Write to Alex Rodriguez

Mr. Alex Rodriguez
c/o The Texas Rangers
The Ballpark in Arlington
1000 Ballpark Way
Arlington, TX 76011

Alex Rodriguez
watches the ball
after he hit it.

WORDS TO KNOW

All-Star team—The top players are picked each year to play for their league in the All-Star Game. The mid-summer classic matches the American League against the National League.

at bat—A player gets an at bat when he comes to the plate and gets a hit, makes an out, or reaches base on an error. He does not get an at bat if he walks, is hit by a pitch, sacrifices, or hits a sacrifice fly.

draft—A selection of players by major-league teams, which take turns choosing the players they want.

free agent—A player who is free to sign with any team.

major leagues—The American League and National League make up the top professional leagues in baseball.

minor leagues—All the pro leagues below the major leagues. Class A is the lowest level. Class AAA is the highest.

playoffs—Following the end of the regular season, four teams from each of the American and National Leagues compete for the World Series championship.

Players Choice Awards—Each year major leaguers vote to decide who is the best player in their league. That player is given the Player of the Year award.

shortstop—The position is part of the "middle infield" with the second baseman. The shortstop usually has the strongest arm of all the infielders.

READING ABOUT

Books

Buckley, Jr., James. *Super Shortstops: Jeter, Nomar, & A-Rod.* New York: Dorling Kindersley Publishing, Inc., 2001.

Christensen, Joe. *Alex Rodriguez.* Edina, Minn.: Abdo Publishers, 2003.

Christopher, Matt and Glenn Stout. *On The Field With Alex Rodriguez.* Boston: Little, Brown Children's Books, 2002.

Covert, Kim. *Alex Rodriguez.* Minnetonka, Minn.: Capstone Press, 2002.

Internet Addresses

The Official Site of Major League Baseball
<http://mlb.com>

The Official Site of the Texas Rangers
<http://texas.rangers.mlb.com/NASApp/mlb/index.jsp?c_id=tex>

INDEX